Living in the Extreme

Lisa Trumbauer

Contents

Rigby®
A Harcourt Achieve Imprint

www.Rigby.com
1-800-531-5015

Where We Live

What is it like where you live? Is your home part of a neighborhood or an apartment complex? Do you live out in the country or in a small town? How far away are the libraries, shopping centers, schools, or grocery stores?

Most people live in communities that provide the basic things they need.

Most people choose to live in places where they can get the things they need. The basic needs for people are housing, food, and clothing. But people also need communities where they can find places to learn, have fun, and work.

Not all people feel the need to live in a city or a bigger community. Some people choose to live in areas that are difficult to get to. They have found ways to get the things they need in some of the most extreme places on Earth.

This picture shows how many people live in New York City.

A home on top of a mountain is not the easiest place to live, nor is a home in the middle of the desert. In places like these, the nearest place where other people live can be many miles away. Traveling can be slow and difficult, especially when the weather is bad.

Living on top of a mountain might not be so easy.

Living in the Arctic

Do you like windy and cold weather? Then living in the Arctic might be the right place for you. The Arctic has some of the most extreme weather on Earth. In the summer, the temperature may get as high as 59 degrees Fahrenheit. In the winter, it can be as cold as −31 degrees Fahrenheit!

The Arctic is one of the most extreme environments on Earth.

Days in the Arctic are very different, too. Because of the way Earth is tilted in space, the Arctic has some very long and very short days. In some places, the sun doesn't shine at all from mid-December to mid-January. But summer days have 24 hours of complete sunlight!

The Arctic is the area around the North Pole.

Arctic Communities

Even under these extreme conditions, people still live in the Arctic. They have found creative ways to enjoy the Arctic weather and make the Arctic their home.

You won't find big cities in the Arctic, but you will find small communities. Just like other communities, the Arctic has areas with homes, schools, and stores.

Homes must be built differently in the Arctic. Because the top layer of ground is **permafrost**, not soil and grass, homes are built on stilts rather than directly on the ground. If they were built directly on ground, the heat from the buildings would melt the frozen ground beneath, and the buildings would sink into the ground.

Buildings in the Arctic are built on stilts so they don't sink into the permafrost.

Kids of the Arctic

Imagine if your community had winter almost all year long. That's what it's like for kids in the Arctic. They must wear heavy clothing most of the time to stay warm. They enjoy many winter sports such as skating, sledding, and hockey, but even sports like basketball are played in the Arctic.

These kids in the Arctic are enjoying a game of basketball.

Would you like to live in the Arctic? How would your life be different from where you live now? What kinds of clothes would you wear? What would you do for fun?

Living in the Desert

The desert is another of Earth's extreme places. Deserts are different from other places in that they get very little rain or snow. Some deserts may be cold, but most deserts are hot and dry. In some deserts, temperatures can be over 100 degrees Fahrenheit. Animals and plants have learned to live in the harsh desert climate, but what about people?

Saguaro cactus

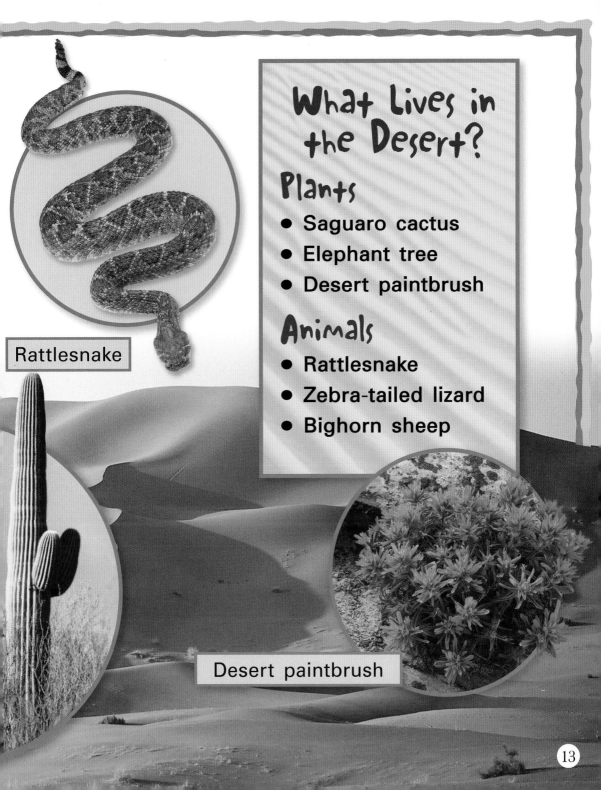

Rattlesnake

What Lives in the Desert?

Plants

- Saguaro cactus
- Elephant tree
- Desert paintbrush

Animals

- Rattlesnake
- Zebra-tailed lizard
- Bighorn sheep

Desert paintbrush

People who live in the desert must learn to live with the desert's heat. Because the desert has few trees, there is very little shade. So people learn to drink lots of water and stay out of the sun during the hottest part of the day. The hottest part of the day is usually from 12:00 P.M. to 4:00 P.M.

Another problem people face in the desert is the lack of water. However, if people dig deep enough underground, they can find water there.

Sometimes people that live in the desert count on machines to help them bring water from far away to their communities.

Native Americans have lived in America's deserts for hundreds of years. They have found creative ways to live in the heat with a lack of water. Some Native Americans have lived at the bottom of **canyons**. Here a river might be found and the air can be cooler. Some Native Americans built homes using wood poles and mud from the surrounding desert.

This Native American home in the desert is made from mud.

Now people often use **adobe** to build their desert homes. They also build their homes in an area where there are breezes. This helps homes stay cooler in the hot weather.

This neighborhood was built using adobe.

Living in the Mountains

Mountaintops can also be extreme places to live. Mountains are often very tall, rocky, and covered with snow. The weather at the top of a mountain is very cool, so the snow here does not melt as quickly as snow at the bottom of a mountain. On some mountaintops, the snow never melts.

The air at the top of a mountain is thinner, or contains less oxygen, than the air at the bottom of a mountain. That means that people living in the mountains have less oxygen to breathe. This can make it harder to breathe when you are hiking, climbing, or even just walking. People who live in such high places must get used to breathing with less oxygen.

People who live in the mountains must get used to living in the thinner air.

The highest mountains in the world are found in Nepal in a mountain range called the Himalayas. People have lived there for many years. They have adapted to mountain living. The thin mountain air doesn't bother them as much as it does newcomers to the area. They are also more able to walk the uneven mountain land.

Many villages in Nepal change the land to fit their needs. They carve out **terraces** of flat, leveled land out of the steep mountainside. The flat land can then be used for farming.

The villagers in Landruk, Nepal, use terrace farming to grow their crops.

Extreme Hotels

Would you like to experience living in an extreme place for a night? You can! Some unusual hotels around the world allow you to live in extreme places for a short time.

The Ice Hotel in Quebec City, Canada, is a place many people like to visit for a unique living experience. In the winter, workers create this hotel out of ice and snow. You can stay in a room made of ice and sleep on an ice bed!

When you stay at the Ice Hotel, you can even sleep on a bed made of ice!

How do you think it would feel to live under the sea? You can stay underwater overnight at a special hotel in Florida. The Jules' Undersea Lodge is a home under the sea. From your window, you can watch the fish and other ocean life swim by. The lodge lets you experience extreme living, if only for a night.

When staying at the Jules' Undersea Lodge, guests can see under water right from their hotel room window.

Glossary

adobe bricks made of dried earth

canyons deep valleys

permafrost frozen ground

terraces steps cut out of the mountainside, making flat land for farming